MEN-AT-ARMS SERIES

EDITOR: MARTIN WINDROW

Army of the Potomac

Text by

PHILIP R. N. KATCHER

Colour plates by

MICHAEL YOUENS

OSPREY PUBLISHING LONDON

Published in 1975 by
Osprey Publishing Ltd
Member company of the George Philip Group
12–14 Long Acre, London WC2E 9LP
© Copyright 1975 Osprey Publishing Ltd
Reprinted 1984, 1985, 1986, 1987

ISBN 0 85045 208 2

Filmset in Great Britain
Printed in Hong Kong

INTRODUCTION

'The defeated troops commenced pouring into Washington over the Long Bridge at daylight on Monday, 22 – day drizzling all through with rain.' [So the poet Walt Whitman watched men of the Union Army return from Bull Run, that battle which was supposed to end the war before it even got a chance to begin.]

'The Saturday and Sunday of the battle [20, 21 July 1861] had been parched and hot to an extreme – the dust, the grime and smoke, in layers, sweated in, followed by other layers again sweated in, absorbed by those excited souls – their clothes all saturated with the clay powder filling the air – stirred up everywhere on the dry roads and trodden fields by the regiments, swarming wagons, artillery, etc. – all the men with this coating of murk and sweat and rain, now recoiling back, pouring over the Long Bridge – a horrible march of twenty miles, returning to Washington baffled, humiliated, panic-struck. Where are the vaunts, and the proud boasts with which you went forth? Where are your banners, and your bands of music and your ropes to bring back your prisoners? Well, there isn't a band playing – and there isn't a flag but clings ashamed and lank to its staff.

'The sun rises, but shines not. The men appear, at first sparsely and shamefaced enough, then thicker, in the streets of Washington – appear in Pennsylvania Avenue, and on the steps and basement entrances. They come along in disorderly mobs, some in squads, stragglers, companies. Occasionally, a rare regiment, in perfect order, with its officers (some gaps, dead, the true braves) marching in silence, with lowering faces, stern, weary to sinking, all black and dirty, but every man with his musket, and stepping alive; but these are the exceptions.'
The army which had gone forth to so easily capture Richmond had met its equal and been turned back. One veteran later said that once getting the order to retreat at Bull Run he would not have stopped retreating until he reached his home town of Boston, Massachusetts, except he was stopped by an armed guard after crossing the Long Bridge into Washington. Now the mob which had been so badly beaten would have to be transformed into an army.

The raw material, the men, was there. It would simply take training, equipping and organizing to convert them from the mob of Bull Run to the Army of the Potomac. A new general, straight from some small victories in western Virginia, George B. McClellan, was brought in to organize and lead the army. In October 1861 the Army of the Potomac officially came into being.

The Men and their Regiment

Before this there was, of course, the regular U.S. Army. In March 1861 it was made up of 13,000 all ranks, and during the war another 67,000 men

A Connecticut regiment's informal camp in early 1861. Note the havelocks, white cap coverings designed to prevent sunstroke, which were quickly abandoned

Major-General George B. McClellan, sixth from left, confers with President Abraham Lincoln after the Battle of Antietam

were recruited for its ranks. Rather than split up the regulars and send them to the volunteer regiments, the army was kept intact, to form a sort of dependable 'old guard' of totally reliable troops. Many regular officers, however, had resigned to accept commissions in the Confederate Army – the men weren't given the chance to do so – while others took higher commissions in volunteer organizations, which meant that regular units were generally under-officered.

The idea of using regulars in this way was probably a successful one, although there was some ill feeling between the regulars and volunteers. The regulars regarded the volunteers as little more than an undisciplined mob, while the volunteers considered the regulars as social inferiors. Nevertheless, when serving together the two types of troops grew to respect each other.

In the meantime, the sight of regulars in action was an inspiration to many volunteers. Wrote one volunteer in 1862: 'Oh, father, how splendidly the

regulars drill; it is perfectly sickening and disgusting to get back here and see our regiment and officers maneuver, after seeing those West Pointers and those veterans of eighteen years' service go through guard mounting.... I am only glad I saw, for now I know I am a better soldier after seeing them perform.'

It was not only in drilling that the regulars looked more soldierly than the new volunteers. Years of learning how to remake government-issue uniforms gave them a real edge in looking smarter. Massachusetts volunteer private Warren Lee Goss wrote: 'My first uniform was a bad fit: my trousers were too long by three or four inches; the flannel shirt was coarse and unpleasant, too large at the neck and too short elsewhere. The forage cap was an ungainly bag with pasteboard top and leather visor; the blouse was the only part which seemed decent; while the overcoat made me feel like a little nubbin of corn [maize] in a large preponderance of husk. Nothing except

"Virginia mud" ever took down my ideas of military pomp quite so low.'

Goss's experiences were hardly unique. The regimental historian of the 8th Vermont Regiment wrote that 'it was clear that Uncle Sam's contracting tailor who made the garments had no idea of measuring the man and then fitting his suit; he seemed rather to expect that, having made the uniforms according to certain patterns, it would be the duty of the officers who distributed them to fit each wearer to his clothes. . . . As a fact, however, when the time came to exchange the citizen's dress for the soldier's garb, it provoked a deal of hilarious mirth to see the square-shouldered, portly man struggling to encase his ample limbs in trousers scant enough to please a dude; while a lean, light-weight comrade fairly lost his corporeal identity in the baggy capacity of a fat man's coat. Nor were the seams of these new garments always equal to the strain to which they were subjected, so that in the course of the first week after they were donned, many of the wearers had to resort to the spools and cushions thoughtfully provided by a loving wife or mother, and turn bushelman.'

Those with uniforms, however, were considered lucky. The 8th Ohio, mustered in late April, did not receive any uniforms until late July. All during that time they carried '. . . wooden guns, wooden swords, and cornstalks with which to drill and mount guard'.

This raw recruit has folded down the standing collar of his frock-coat so his tie and paper collar show

The Infantry Regiment

Once the men were gathered into units, uniformed, accoutred and armed, they had to be organized into formal units conforming to official regulations. A regular infantry regiment was made up of two or more battalions of eight companies each. Organization of the volunteer infantry regiments was to be different. Each regiment was to consist of ten companies, each with a captain, a first lieutenant, a second lieutenant, a first (or orderly) sergeant, four sergeants, eight corporals, two musicians, a waggoner, and eighty-two privates. Each company was divided into two

This corporal wears the dark blue trousers originally ordered for the army, but soon changed to the pre-war sky-blue

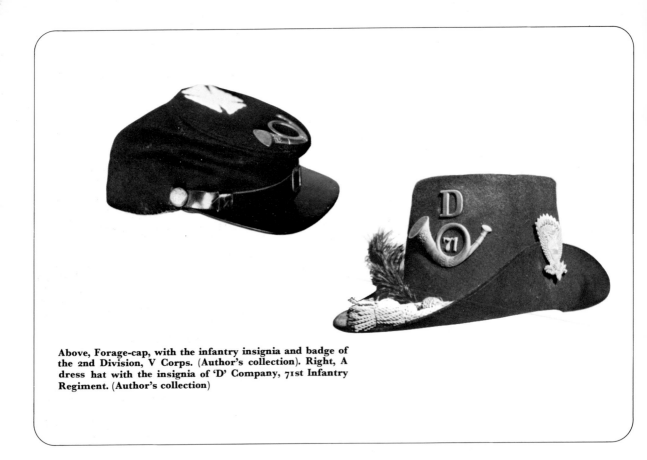

Above, Forage-cap, with the infantry insignia and badge of the 2nd Division, V Corps. (Author's collection). Right, A dress hat with the insignia of 'D' Company, 71st Infantry Regiment. (Author's collection)

platoons, and each platoon into two sections. The regiment itself also included a colonel, a lieutenant-colonel, a major, a lieutenant holding the post of adjutant, another lieutenant as quartermaster, a surgeon and his assistant. Non-commissioned ranks on the regimental staff included a sergeant-major, a quartermaster-sergeant, a commissary sergeant, a hospital steward, two principal musicians and twenty-four bandsmen. The bandsmen were later authorized only on brigade level.

Actually, due to the difficulty of recruiting when away from the state and losses in the field, strengths were usually under regulation. On the average, an infantry regiment at Fair Oaks in 1862 had some 650 men, while at Chancellorsville, May 1863, it had 530 men. The average regiment at Gettysburg, July 1863, had 375 men, and at the Wilderness, 1864, 440 men. Eventually 1,696 regiments of infantry were recruited into the Union Army.

In action, the regiment sent a company or two some 400 to 500 yards ahead of the main body to act as skirmishers. The rest of the regiment was drawn up, two lines deep, with, at times, a company or two held behind the lines for a reserve. As the war progressed and it was seen how the deadly accurate rifled musket ruled out the tactics of Wellington and Washington, it became the practice to send out about half the regiment in skirmish line – an informal line where men hid behind whatever cover they could find and fired independently of command. The rest of the regiment was actually held in reserve.

On the attack, regiments were moved forward in waves, with some 250 to 300 yards between them, so that stray shots aimed at the first wave would not hit the second.

Regiments themselves were usually made up of people from the same area, although the diversity of the northern population meant a wide variety of backgrounds would be found in the same regiment. An élite unit, the 5th New York, had a Company 'B' made up, for example, of sixty-seven native New Yorkers, eight men from other states,

A whole regiment performs a rarely used tactic, forming a square against cavalry

thirty-five Irish, eighteen Germans, fourteen Englishmen, five Canadians, four Scotsmen and three Frenchmen. Company 'C', 2nd New York Heavy Artillery, boasted sixty-two different professions in its ranks, ranging from 'speculator' to 'gold beater' and from 'wool stapler' to 'reporter'.

Most regiments had distinctive characters. The 15th Wisconsin, commanded by Colonel Hans Heg, was almost wholly Norwegian, while Frenchmen went into the 55th New York (Gardes Lafayette) and Poles into the 58th New York (Polish Legion). Actually, most non-American-born men who went into the army were Germans, followed closely by the Irish. More than 50,000 Canadians and 45,000 Englishmen, with a large number of Scotsmen and Welsh, also found their way into Union ranks.

One regiment, the 79th New York (Cameron Highlanders), was almost wholly Scottish, and went to war behind the pipes, all the men in kilts and bonnets. The kilts lasted only as far as from New York to Washington, where they were put into storage, but the men then wore trews of the Cameron tartan, and kept their bonnets throughout the war.

Men felt more pride in their regiments than in their brigades, divisions, or even corps – although later the corps became a focal point for pride as well. A private of the 1st Massachusetts wrote in April 1862: 'I had rather be a private in the Mass. 1st regiment than to hold the highest commision in any of the others, and I have heard many say the same.' One who didn't say the same about the 1st Massachusetts was a sergeant of the 1st Minnesota, after Fredericksburg, when he wrote: 'I would rather be a private in this regiment than captain in any that I know of.'

These were men in what would be considered ordinary infantry regiments. Some regiments were unique to begin with and, if possible, even more proud of themselves – the zouave regiments. The first zouaves were a tribe of Berbers in Algeria of that name who were recruited into the French Army in 1831. They were dressed in great

Zouaves on the attack

baggy trousers, with short jackets and fezzes and turbans. Later, Frenchmen themselves joined zouave units, and their Crimean War exploits and unique drill caused them to be widely copied in the U.S.

The true, full zouave uniform included a red felt fez skull-cap, with a long wool worsted string hanging from the centre of the cap's top and ending in a large, coarse worsted tassel. The cap was worn by itself in the field, but for parade a flannel turban, about 1 foot wide and 10 feet long, was wound round the fez. Short waistcoats were worn, which were often false and simply fronts sewn into the jackets. The jackets themselves were short, usually blue with red flannel trim all over them. They were often hooked-and-eyed shut at the throat while the rest of the jacket was worn open.

A giant flannel sash, about the same size as the turban, was worn round the waist and under the waist-belt.

Trousers were enormous wool, baggy things, usually red or blue. They were tucked into leggings,

canvas or leather, which covered the shoe-tops and came up halfway to the knees.

Such may have been a uniform to provoke pride in the wearer, but outsiders often cast a jaundiced eye on it. An old regular army general was walking near the camp of a newly arrived New York zouave regiment, when one of their officers saluted him. Instead of returning the salute, the general stared at him in apparent amazement.

'Who are you?'

'I'm a zouave.'

'What is that?'

'An officer of a zouave regiment, sir.'

'An officer! I thought you were a circus clown.'

Actually, zouave officers rarely wore the full uniform their men did. Usually they wore the same coat other officers did, with a gold-trimmed red *kepi* and trousers cut to the normal cut but of the same colour as their men's.

Not all the units bearing the name of 'zouaves', however, arrayed themselves in this full glory. Lew Wallace, colonel commanding Wallace's

8

Zouaves, the 11th Indiana, wrote about his unit: 'There was nothing of the flashy, Algerian colors in the uniform . . . no red fez . . . no red breeches, no red or yellow sash with tassels big as early cabbages. Our outfit was of the tamest gray twilled goods, not unlike home-made jeans, and a visor cap, French in pattern, its top of red cloth not larger than the palm of one's hand; a blue flannel shirt with open neck; a jacket, Greekish in form, edges with narrow binding . . . breeches baggy, but not petticoated; button gaiters connecting below the knees with the breeches, and strapped over the shoe.'

Typically, regiments which began the war in zouave outfits found them too conspicuous in action, hard to care for and replace, and generally not suited for active service. The 95th Pennsylvania (Gosline's Zouaves), for example, began the war in October 1861 with red trousers, brown leather leggings, short blue jackets with brass ball buttons and blue shirts, both jacket and shirt being heavily trimmed with red braid. By 1862, however, this distinguished uniform began to disappear, to be replaced with the standard infantry fatigue uniform.

Still, people were pleased with the appearance of zouave uniforms and they didn't want them to die out all together. A private of the 140th New York wrote home in January 1864 that 'it has been rumored for a long time that the 140th were to have zouave uniforms and yesterday the expectation was realized . . . the pants are bag style, gathered at the waist and ankles. A short jacket – made so as to represent jacket and vest together – red trimmings on the breast, and bound with the same color. A blue sash around the waist, bound with red. The cap has a large blue tassel . . . this will hereafter be the 140th N.Y. Zouaves.' From an original uniform it would appear the 140th's uniforms were imported from France, although in April 1863 Colonel Kenner Gerrard of the 146th New York was sent to Washington to supervise the manufacture of zouave uniforms for his regiment there.

A special addition to many zouave units were *vivandières* – women in dress similar to the men's – who carried kegs filled with water (or hard spirits) to pass out to the men. Most of these, too, lasted only a short time, but not all. An officer of the 8th Ohio, heavily engaged in fighting at the Bloody Angle in 1864, wrote: 'At one time the shower of musket-balls, shrapnel, and every sort of projectile falling in the midst of us was trying to the nerves of our coolest. Just then I heard a man calling, "Annie, come this way." To hear a woman's name at such a time was rather startling. I looked around. Sure enough, there was a woman! She was about twenty-five years of age, square-featured and sun-burnt, and dressed in Zouave uniform in the Vivandière style. She was with two men and they seemed to be looking for their regiment, the 114th Pennsylvania Infantry, they said, which was also known as the Collis Zouaves. Hers was the only face in the vicinity which seemed in any way gay. She was laughing and pointing very unconcernedly, as she stumbled over axes, spades, and other obstacles, on her way through the trench! She was wonderfully courageous or else she did not understand the danger.'

Besides the zouaves, volunteer regiments began the war in a wide variety of uniforms. Some were pre-war militia units, who had their old uniforms, such as the 7th New York State Militia. According to a veteran in 1863 they were wearing, even that long after the start of the war, '. . . their gorgeous uniforms, gray with gilt trimmings and patent-leather belts and knapsacks . . .'. Gray was, in fact, the most common colour chosen for volunteers, which created problems in battle where the enemy also wore gray. They had to get rid of the gray uniforms.

Enlisted men's brass shoulder-scales, worn for dress. (Author's collection)

This young soldier wears his forage-cap and issue trousers, coloured sky-blue on the original tintype, but his checked shirt and trimmed waistcoat are definitely items brought from home, as was common among both officers and enlisted men. (Author's collection)

The 3rd Maine was among those issued gray uniforms but, wrote an officer of the regiment, after reaching Washington: '. . . July 3d we gave up the gray regimentals that we had worn from home, and received new uniforms; loose blue flannel blouses, looser light-blue pantaloons, and baggy forage caps; not a fit in the lot.'

The infantryman's regulation dress uniform was actually a rather smart one. It consisted of a black felt hat, 6¼ inches tall, and pinned up on the left side with a brass, stamped eagle. A sky-blue worsted cord was worn round the crown, ending in two tassels in front and holding a black ostrich feather on the right side. A large brass *Jäger* [or hunter] horn was on the front, in the middle of which was the man's brass regimental number. An inch-tall brass letter, worn on top of the horn, marked his company.

The coat was dark blue wool, reaching almost to the knees. According to regulations, it was '. . . without plaits, with a skirt ending one-half

the distance from the top of the hip to the bend of the knee; one row of nine buttons on the breast, placed at equal distances; stand-up collar to rise no higher than to permit the chin to turn freely over it, to hook in front at the bottom and then to slope up and backward at a 30-degree angle on each side; cuffs pointed . . . and to button with two small buttons at the under seams; collar and cuffs edged with a cord or welt of [sky-blue] cloth . . .'. A brass shoulder-scale was to be worn on each shoulder.

Although the coats were fairly popular, especially for dress, the hats were rarely worn. One soldier wrote home: 'My new hat looks near like the pictures that you see of the Pilgrim Fathers landing on Plymouth, tall, stiff and turned up on one side with a feather on it . . . I don't wear it any more than I am obliged to.'

Trousers were heavy sky-blue wool. They were, according to the regulations in effect when the war began, the same dark blue as the coats; however, on 16 December 1861, the colour was changed to sky-blue which it had been before. Only a few dark blue trousers are seen in period photographs, and all from early ones. Trousers were made cuffless, with a small slit on each outside leg seam. They were held up by braces, with white metal buttons on the outside of the trousers for the braces, and no belt loops. They also lacked back pockets, and only had two deep front pockets.

Shirts were generally gray flannel. Underclothes were tan-coloured and long. One Indiana soldier wrote: 'Most of the boys had never worn drawers and some did not know what they were for and some of the old soldiers who are here told them they were for an extra uniform to be worn on parade and they half believed it.'

According to another veteran: 'There was little attempt made to repair the socks drawn from the government supplies, for they were generally of the shoddiest description and not worth it. In symmetry, they were like the elbow of a stove pipe; nor did the likeness end here, for while the stove pipe is open at both ends, so were the socks within forty-eight hours after putting them on.'

Boots, or shoes, were square-toed, black and cut for the right and left feet – among the first mass-produced in America to be so cut. Called 'mudscows' and 'gun boats' by the men, they were cut just to about the ankle-bone. Many were of such poor quality as to last only twenty to thirty days, while some soles were so thin as to be wearable only on dry ground. An Ohio officer reported in early 1863: 'My feet are very sore, for I am now almost barefooted. When leaving Gettysburg, I had got myself a pair of shoes which were much too large. As I have been compelled from time to time to slash them with my knife, and, as the edges of the slashed leather chafe, I have again cut away the uppers until my shoes look like nothing but sandals.' By 18 July he noted: 'I am barefooted. Long ago I threw away the shoes which I got at Gettysburg. A good part of our marching is on mountain roads, made of sharp-cornered broken stone, or through the open wastes on the side of mountains, where the briars and blackberry bushes cut my feet at every step. But I have plenty of company. Almost half of us are barefooted now.'

On fatigue duties and in the field the black felt hat and frock-coat were replaced with the fatigue uniform. The cap was dark blue wool with a cardboard stiffening on top. Two brass side buttons held the leather chinstrap, which also had a brass buckle. The lining was of polished cotton, usually brown, with a leather sweatband and visor. The visor was also lacquered black. The same horn, number and letter were often worn on the cap's board top as were worn on the hat's front.

The fatigue blouse was described as a 'sack coat'. According to regulations it was 'of dark blue flannel, extending half the distance down the thigh, and made loose without body or sleeve lining, falling collar, inside pocket on the left side, four coat buttons down the front'. Recruits were to receive their sack coat, '. . . made with sleeve and body lining, the latter of flannel'.

This uniform was typical of most infantry privates in the Army of the Potomac. A major, commanding one of the army's regiments, described the typical, 'Portrait of a private'. 'The ideal picture of a soldier makes a veteran smile. Be a man never so much a man, his importance and conceit dwindle when he crawls into an unteaseled shirt, trousers too short and very baggy behind, coat too long at both ends, shoes with soles like firkin covers, and a cap as shapeless as a feed bag.

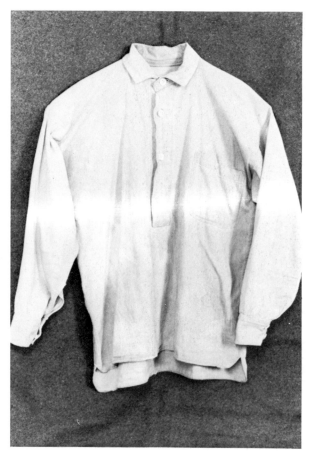

Period issue shirt. (Author's collection)

Let me recall how our private looked to me in the army, in the ranks, a position he chose from pure patriotism. I can see him exactly as I saw him then. He is just in front of me trying to keep his balance and his temper, as he spews from a dry mouth the infernally fine soil of Virginia, and with his hands – he hasn't a handkerchief – wipes the streaks of dirty sweat that make furrows down his unshaven face. No friend of civilian days would recognize him in this most unattractive and disreputable-looking fellow, bowed under fifty-eight pounds of army essentials. . . .

'His suit is a model one, cut after the regulation pattern, fifty thousand at a time, and of just two sizes. If he is a small man, God pity him; and if he is a big man, God pity him still more; for he is an object of ridicule. His forage cap, with its leather visor, when dry, curls up, when wet hangs down, and usually covers one or both ears. His army brogans, nothing can ever make shine, or even black. Perhaps the coat of muddy blue can be

The 1st U.S. Coloured Troops, recruited in the Washington, D.C., area, fought in the Petersburg, Va., area battles. (Black Spear Historical Productions)

buttoned in front, and it may be lapped and buttoned behind. The tailor never bushels army suits, and he doesn't crease trousers, although he is always generous in reinforcing them with the regulation patch.

'The knapsack [which is cut to fit, in the engraving] is an unwieldy burden with its rough, coarse contents of flannel and sole leather and sometimes twenty rounds of ammunition extra. Mixed in with these regulation essentials, like beatitudes, are photographs, cards, 'housewife', Testament, pens, ink, paper. All this is crowned with a double wool blanket and half a shelter tent rolled in a rubber blanket. One shoulder and the hips support the "commissary department" – an odorous haversack, which often stinks with its mixture of bacon, pork, salt junk, sugar, coffee, tea, desiccated vegetables, rice, bits of yesterday's dinner, and old scraps husbanded with miserly care against a day of want sure to come.

'Loaded down, in addition, with a canteen, full cartridge-box, belt, crossbelt, and musket,

and tramping twenty miles in a hurry on a hot day, our private was a soldier, but not just then a praiser of the soldier's life. I saw him multiplied by thousands.'

Personal Equipment

Knapsacks were of canvas, tarred to make them waterproof. They were made with two sections inside, in which clothes and whatever else could be stored. The soldier's gray or brown blanket was rolled up and strapped on top of the whole knapsack. The knapsack was carried by two large leather straps, which were divided into two smaller straps about the middle of the chest. One set of the smaller straps were attached to the knapsack's bottom, while the other had a set of brass hooks. These were designed to be attached to keeps on a special waist-belt, but this waist-belt was virtually never issued. Instead, the

A company of the 6th Maine Regiment. Note the corps badges on their forage-caps

soldiers either hooked them to their regular waist-belts or across their chests. Either way the knapsack was uncomfortable to wear.

So uncomfortable, in fact, that at the Battle of Chancellorsville some 25 per cent of the entire Army of the Potomac claimed to have 'lost' their knapsacks. Instead, the men rolled up their blanket and waterproof or shelter half, with their clothes inside, and wore them round their bodies, horse-collar fashion.

If knapsacks weren't lost, they were quite often left somewhere while the army went into the field. An Ohio soldier, just before Antietam, wrote: 'They are issuing us shoes and fresh ammunition. We are very dirty and very lousy. The shirts we have on our backs now, we have worn for about a month. As our knapsacks are stored somewhere in Washington or Alexandria [Virginia], there is little hope of changing our shirts until some very desperate or important movements have been made. We all scratch alike, generals and privates.'

Each man received a waterproof, or rubber

blanket. A Massachusetts veteran described them as being '. . . made of unbleached muslin coated with vulcanized India rubber, sixty inches wide and seventy-one inches long, having an opening in the center lengthwise of the poncho, through which the head passes, with a lap three inches wide and sixteen inches long'. The uncoated side of these was often drawn on, usually making a board for dice games.

The other such item carried was the shelter half. It was usually made of cotton drilling, about 5 feet 2 inches long by 4 feet 8 inches wide. Each one had a row of buttonholes and buttons on three sides and a pair of holes for stake loops in each corner. Every two men were to share shelter halfs, and two, together, would make a small tent, then called a 'dog' or 'shelter' tent. Often three men would go together to make a larger, fancier tent.

Haversacks differed greatly. The issue one generally was a blackened canvas bag – treated like the knapsack to make it waterproof – some 13 inches long, $12\frac{1}{2}$ inches wide and carried on a

George M. Stevens, private, 'H' Company, 9th New Hampshire Infantry 2nd Brigade, 2nd Division, IX Corps, holds a Model 1841 rifle with its wicked sabre bayonet. He died in service July 1863. (Author's collection)

Left, The issue haversack. (Author's collection). Right, Typical Union Army canteen, carried by W. Dunn, 'M' Company, 1st Maine Heavy Artillery. (Author's collection)

32-inch-long strap. It was buckled shut with a single strap on its centre and often a tin canteen cup was carried with its handle buckled on the haversack strap.

Inside the haversack was another canvas bag, the same size as the haversack and held in place by three buttons. This was issued as a separate food bag, but was often cut up for gun patches. Though they started white in colour, as a veteran wrote: 'By the time one of these had been in use for a few weeks as a receptacle for chunks of fat bacon and fresh meat, damp sugar tied up in a rag – perhaps a piece of an old shirt – potatoes and other vegetables that might be picked up along the route, it took on the color of a printing office towel. It would have been alike offensive to the eyes and nose of a fastidious person.'

The haversack hung on the soldier's left side. On top of that he hung his waterbottle, or canteen. This was made of tin, covered in wool, gray, brown, light or dark blue, with a white cotton strap. It held $1\frac{1}{4}$ quarts of water. The mouth was

of pewter, and it had a chain running between one of the sling loops and the stopper. The stopper was cork, with a tin cap on top and a washer on the bottom and a metal rod, bent into a circle on top, running through it. The pewter top was unfortunate, as it dented easily, and water could splash out of a full canteen on the march and run down the haversack and trouser leg.

Canteens were often marked with the soldier's name, company letter or regimental designation.

The cartridge-box was made of black leather with two tin containers inside it divided into six areas to hold the paper-wrapped cartridges. Each box contained forty cartridges – forty 'dead men' to the soldiers. The box was originally issued with an oval brass cartridge-box plate attached to the flap to keep it from flying up when the soldier was in action and the flap not fastened. Later boxes were issued with the oval shape and letters 'U.S.' impressed into the leather flap where the plate had gone. State troops often had their state letters on the cartridge-box plates, such as

Left, The brass eagle-plate worn on the cartridge-box sling on the centre of the chest was simply for decoration. (Author's collection). Right, Buff leather waist-belt with brass keeps and the standard belt-plate. The other plate is for the State of New York, and other states generally issued their own designs on the same oval brass plates. (Author's collection)

'N.H.S.M.' (New Hampshire State Militia), 'S.N.Y.' (State of New York), or 'O.V.M.' (Ohio Volunteer Militia). Even regimental designations were sometimes used, like the 'P.F.Z.' (Philadelphia Fire Zouaves).

Inside, a separate underflap, also leather, helped keep the cartridges dry. A small envelope of leather on front of the box held gun patches and some tools.

Usually the box was carried on a black leather sling which was slipped through loops on the back and buckled to two small iron buckles on the bottom of the box. Zouaves carried their boxes through horizontal loops on their waist-belts, and the issue boxes had loops to enable them to be worn either way.

A circular brass plate, bearing an eagle motif, was worn on the crossbelt, just over the centre of the soldier's chest. It, as the cartridge-box and waist-belt plates, was made of thin stamped brass, backed up with lead.

A buff leather belt, dark brown on the outside

and white on the inside, was worn round the waist. Its buckle was an oval brass belt-plate of the same design and size as that on the cartridge-box flap. On the other end, two brass keeps hooked over the belt to keep it neatly in place.

On the right hip, next to the belt-plate, was the small, leather pouch in which the soldier carried the copper caps, filled with fulminate of mercury, used to fire the musket. The cap-box was held on by two loops on the back, and dyed all black. A large flap was fastened to a brass finial at the box's bottom, while a smaller underflap underneath helped keep the caps in when the soldier was in action. The top of the box, too, was filled with a piece of lamb's fleece, also as a retainer for the caps. Inside the box, in a small holder, was a thin wire pick, used to clear out the musket's cone or nipple.

On his left hip the soldier hung his bayonet scabbard, under the haversack and canteen. It too was of black leather, with the frog usually made of buff leather and riveted with copper

Above, The cartridge-box holds two tin containers, each of which carries twenty rounds. (Author's collection). Right, Cap-box and caps. (Author's collection)

rivets. The scabbard was sewn into the frog and had a brass chape. The bayonet in it was 1 foot 6 inches long, made of iron with a steel blade. Triangular in section, it had a socket which slipped round the musket's muzzle and was attached by means of a slit to accommodate the front sight and a locking ring which closed behind the sight.

This complete set of equipment proved quite confusing to the raw recruits of 1861. A Massachusetts volunteer recalled '. . . the first march of any consequence we had taken with our knapsacks and equipments. Our dress consisted of a belt about the body, which held a cartridge-box and bayonet, a crossbelt, also a haversack and tin drinking-cup, a canteen, and, last but not least, the knapsack strapped to the back. The straps ran over, around, and about one, in confusion most perplexing to our unsophisticated shoulders, the knapsack constantly giving the wearer the feeling that he was being pulled over backward. My canteen banged against my bayonet, both tin cup and bayonet badly interfered with the butt of my musket, while my cartridge-box and haversack were constantly flopping up and down – the whole jangling like loose harness and chains on a runaway horse.'

Although soldiers did get used to wearing the entire kit, they were never really happy about it. Several years later another veteran wrote home: 'In addition to the actual weight the five different straps which passed over every part of our bodies produced unpleasant touches of cramp now & then. I can appreciate the feelings of an animal in harness now.'

After receiving this vast store of accoutrements, new recruits were just about ready to receive anything. Quickly the story made the rounds of the new recruit who just received his uniform and accoutrements and returned to his tent with them. After looking them over, an old soldier in his squad asked why he didn't receive his umbrella. 'Oh,' naïvely asked the recruit, 'do they furnish an umbrella?'

'Certainly,' replied the veteran. 'It's just like

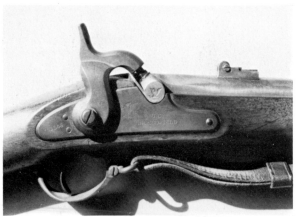

Lock-plate of the second 1863 pattern, Springfield rifled musket, the standard weapon of the war. (Author's collection)

officer of the Inspector-General's office as being mostly '. . . drunken ragged soldiers in the streets, and dirty officers about the hotels. . . . Many cases of officers and enlisted men wearing the gray pants of the rebel service . . . some enlisted men entirely dressed in rebel colors.'

Even if at times uniforms were hard to get, the government made sure everyone was armed.

Weapons and Insignia

that fraud of a quartermaster to cheat a recruit out of a part of his outfit. Go back and *demand* your umbrella.'

The recruit probably learned quickly what the official quartermaster view on umbrellas was. Indeed, at periods in the war he would be quite lucky to receive even necessary items, especially on a long campaign. A member of a regiment just returned from the unsuccessful Valley campaign in May 1862 confided in his diary that 'by now we look like a pack of thieving vagabonds – no crowns in our hats, no soles to our shoes, no seats to our pantaloons. We make a good foil to the sleek, well-fed soldiers of McDowell's corps who are occupying Fredericksburg.' Troops stationed away from the main army had the hardest time drawing necessary supplies. Troops near Cumberland, Maryland, in 1864 were reported by an

The basic infantry weapon was the muzzle-loading, single-shot Minié rifled musket, Model 1861. It fired a 0·58-calibre bullet, called a Minié ball after its French inventor, carried in a rolled paper cartridge with sixty grains of black powder. The ball was conical in shape, expanding when the powder was fired to grip the three-groove rifling in the barrel. The musket was capable of hitting an 11-inch bull's-eye at 333 yards, and at 500 yards could penetrate about 6 inches of pine. The Union Army between 1861 and 1865 acquired 1,472,614 of these rifled muskets, including the only slightly changed models of 1863 and 1863A or 1864.

The first job was to arm people quickly, however, and therefore muskets were bought outside the U.S. The most popular of these was the British Army's Enfield rifled musket, which fired a 0·577 Minié ball and was virtually the same as the Springfield. It had brass furniture, unlike the iron Springfield furniture, and a more elaborate sight and nipple protector, but lacked the interchangeability of parts which was an important feature of the 1861 Springfield. The government bought 428,292 Enfields.

The 20th Maine received Enfields, but after Gettysburg they gathered six mule-loads of captured muskets from the field – including Springfields by the score – and exchanged their Enfields for Springfields. A corporal in the regiment said the Enfields shot as well, but the Maine men thought them hard to take care of and the Springfields would require half the time and work to keep clean.

Mounted man's belt-plate. The wreath is of silver, the rest brass. (Author's collection)

Other muskets, more disliked than Enfields, were bought from Austria, Belgium and France, along with other European states. Even old smoothbore muskets were hauled out of stores and issued. In 1861 the 13th Pennsylvania Reserves (the Bucktail Rifles) were issued 1837 0·69-calibre smoothbore muskets and some of the men absolutely refused to accept them. They were a *rifle* regiment and had been promised Minié rifles!

Probably one of the greatest sins committed against the men in blue by their own government was being issued single-shot, muzzle-loading muskets when fine multiple-shot, breech-loading weapons were available. The old, conservative Ordnance head felt the magazine weapons were too expensive, while the men would shoot wildly with too much ammunition, which would cost the taxpayer more.

The fact is, however, men with only one shot tended to use it quicker, with less aim, so they could reload quicker, while those with magazine-fed weapons could aim and fire under less pressure. Then, too, any muzzle-loader lost to the rebels would be put into service against Union troops, while the South was unable until very, very late in the war to make the brass cartridge-cases needed for magazine weapons.

The soldiers themselves, however, were determined to acquire modern weapons, even if the Ordnance Department was against it. One infantryman wrote in his diary: 'I got a Henry rifle – a 16 shooter. I gave 35 dollars – all the money I had for it. I am glad I could get it. They are good shooters and I like to think I have so many shots in reserve.' A major wrote of his regiment that 'every man felt confident that with his new Spencer [a seven-shot repeater] he was good for at least any two rebs in Dixie. . . . We think our Spencers saved us, and our men adore them as do the heathen their idols.'

Besides their muskets, non-commissioned officers were marked by another rather obsolete weapon – the sword. The N.C.O. sword was the 1840 pattern, adopted from a French pattern, with a straight blade and all-brass hilt. It was carried in a black leather scabbard, with a brass tip, in a buff leather belt across the left shoulder with a double frog for both sword and bayonet.

Corporals didn't carry swords, and were only

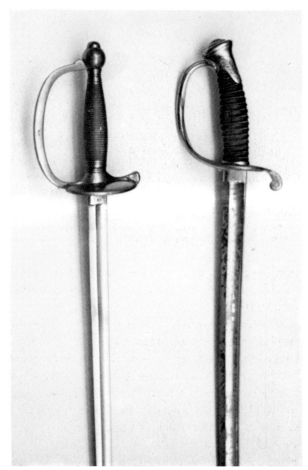

Left, the issue non-commissioned officer's sword, with a straight blade and all-brass hilt and, right, the issue foot officer's sabre, with engraved blade, leather and wire wrapped grip, and engraved brass hilt. (Smithsonian Institution)

marked by two chevrons, points down, in sky-blue worsted for infantry on each sleeve. They also wore an inch-wide dark blue stripe down their trouser legs.

Sergeants, and above, were to carry swords, although very few did in the field. They were further marked by three worsted chevrons and a red worsted sash worn under the waist-belt. The first or orderly sergeant wore a worsted diamond above his three chevrons. The sergeant-major's chevrons were in silk, and featured three chevrons with three arcs above them. All enlisted men who served faithfully for five years wore a diagonal half-chevron, half an inch wide, from seam to seam, on each lower arm of their dress coats. Service in war was marked by a red or sky-blue edging on the service stripe, depending on the man's branch.

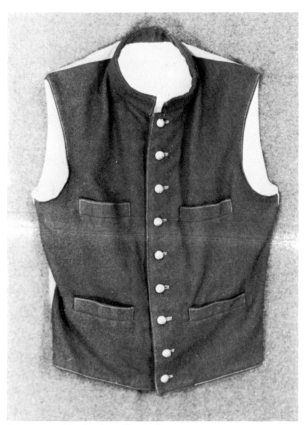

Issue vest. (Author's collection)

Infantry officers carried a 1850-pattern sword, with a slightly curved, engraved blade, in a black leather or blackened iron scabbard. Their sword-belts were fastened with exactly the same belt-plate as that worn by sergeants and all mounted men – a rectangular one featuring a brass coat of arms of the U.S. with a separate silver wreath applied round the outside edge.

The officer's sash was crimson silk and was worn round the waist. The officer of the day was marked by wearing his sash from his right shoulder to his left hip instead of round the waist.

The officer's uniform was also different from the enlisted man's. His coat was a dark blue frock-coat, extending '. . . from two-thirds to three-fourths of the distance from the top of the hip to the bend of the knee'. Captains and lieutenants wore a single row of equally placed buttons. Majors and colonels wore two rows of seven buttons on their coats. While enlisted men's buttons had a plain eagle with a shield on its chest on their buttons, officers had the letter of their corps on the shield on their buttons.

'Generals had buttons with an elaborate eagle with stars around it. Brigadier-generals wore eight buttons, in pairs, in two rows, while major-generals wore two rows of nine buttons each, placed in threes. All of them wore three buttons on each cuff.

'On their shoulders officers were to wear gold epaulettes with a solid gold crescent around the end. Generals wore one or two stars on theirs, depending on rank. Infantry officers wore the number of their regiment embroidered in gold within a circlet of embroidered silver one and three-fourths inches in diameter on sky-blue cloth. A colonel also wore a silver embroidered eagle on his. The lieutenant-colonel had a silver embroidered oak leaf. The major's was plain. Captain's epaulettes were generally smaller and had two silver embroidered bars. The first lieutenant had but one bar and the second lieutenant none.

'In the field shoulder-straps were substituted for epaulettes. They were about an inch and a half wide and four inches long. Generals had black velvet ones, with an embroidered gold edge round the outside and one or two silver stars inside. Infantry officers had gold embroidery edging sky-blue cloth, with an eagle for the colonel, two silver oak leaves for the lieutenant-colonel and two gold oak leaves for the major. The captain had two gold bars at each end of the strap, while the first lieutenant had a single bar at each end and the second lieutenant had empty straps.

'Because large badges often made officers good targets in the field by late in the war, officers often used small metal rank badges worn on their fatigue blouse's laydown collar or on each shoulder.

'The plain soldier's fatigue blouse, as well as short jackets, were quite popular in the field although most officers wore their frock coats.

'Trousers worn by infantry officers were dark blue with a $\frac{1}{8}$ inch welt of sky blue on the outer seam. They were otherwise the same as the other ranks.'

Hats were the same, too. Officers usually had their badges embroidered in gold thread with the regimental number in the centre of an oval of black velvet. In the field officers either wore issue forage-caps or bought copies of the stiff French *kepi*, a smaller cap than the issue forage-cap.

Besides the sword, officers generally carried pistols in the field. The most common pistol of the war was the 0·44-calibre Colt 'Army' revolver, with brass backgrip and all-steel works, or the similar 0·36-calibre Colt 'Navy' revolver. Rhode Island officers, for example, seem to have been issued Colt revolvers with their ranks engraved on the backstraps. Over 100,000 Colt 'Army' revolvers were supplied to the government during the war.

A revolver just about as popular as the Colt was the Remington. It was generally similar, but had a backstrap over the cylinder which made for a generally stronger weapon.

All revolvers of the period tended to have one serious problem – the flash from a round being fired often set off all the other rounds in the cylinder, a practice which could destroy the weapon, and the user's hand with it.

Revolvers, nevertheless, were quite popular with all ranks of another major corps, the artillery. Men for some seventy-eight artillery regiments were recruited and organized by the Union Army.

The Artillery

There were basically two types of artillery – field artillery and heavy artillery. Both were put into regiments which were divided into twelve batteries. Field artillery batteries were usually combined with infantry regiments at brigade level.

Heavy artillery regiments were posted to various fortifications, mostly round the major cities and seaports, with the job of manning the large guns. Some heavy artillery accompanied the main army as specialists manning the army's siege-train, but few of their number saw action. In the final, closing months of the war, when Grant needed every man he could get into the Army of the Potomac, many of the heavy artillerymen were pulled out of Washington's fortifications to serve as infantry – and serve well they did. The 1st Maine Artillery took more casualties in the Wilderness than any other Union regiment in any single action, losing some 600 out of 900 men in one attack of only a few minutes.

Heavy artillerymen had identical uniforms to

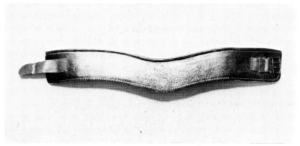

An officer's black leather stock. (Jack Helms collection)

those of the infantry, only N.C.O.s' chevrons, trouser stripes, frock-coat trim, officers' shoulder-straps and hat cords were red, not sky-blue. In addition, each artilleryman was to carry a short (26-inch-long) sword, with an all-brass hilt, which had been copied from a French version of the ancient Roman infantryman's sword. Heavy things with wide blades, they were carried on special buff leather belts. Such weapons saw no action.

Instead of the *Jäger* horns on their hats they wore large brass crossed cannon.

While heavy artillery regiments served together generally, field artillery was mainly used on a battery level. Each battery was made up of six guns, although this was later reduced to four during the Wilderness, commanded by a captain. Two guns were a section, under a lieutenant. Each gun was hooked to a limber, which carried ammunition, while each gun also had a caisson with three more ammunition (or limber) chests on it. Each gun, limber and caisson was a platoon commanded by a sergeant, called the 'chief of the piece'.

Shoulder-straps of, left, a brigadier-general and, right, a first lieutenant. (Author's collection)

This Wisconsin lieutenant wears the regulation officer's frock-coat and shoulder-straps for his rank. Leaving the coat in part unbuttoned was highly fashionable. (Author's collection)

Although usually assigned to brigades by batteries, a large and well-led artillery reserve in the Army of the Potomac made possible massed cannon fire where at places like Malvern Hill it could virtually stop rebel attacks by itself. Indeed, Union artillery was consistently superior to Confederate – man for man and gun for gun – throughout the war. One reason was the superior quality of fuses, powder, shells and artillery pieces.

The pieces most used by field artillery were the 3-inch rifle, the 10-lb Parrot (both rifled iron cannon firing the same ammunition) and the 12-lb Napoleon, a bronze smoothbore cannon. There was considerable debate as to which was the superior weapon, but because artillery had no more of an accurate range than the rifled musket, both were equally dangerous to man on the field.

At Spotsylvania a section of Battery 'C', 5th U.S. Artillery, went into action against rebel infantry, ahead of their own infantry support. 'Of course', wrote a Battery 'C' veteran, 'artillery could not live long under such a fire as the enemy were putting in through there. Our men went down in short order. The left gun fired nine rounds, I fired fourteen with mine. . . . Our section went into action with 23 men and one officer. The only ones who came out sound were the lieutenant and myself. Every horse was killed, 7 of the men were killed outright, 16 wounded [7 men made up a gun crew]; the gun carriages were so cut with bullets as to be of no further service . . . 27 balls passed through the lid of the limber chest while number six [cannoneers were known by their position numbers] was getting out ammunition. The sponge bucket on my gun had 39 holes in it being perforated like a sieve.'

Besides their cannon, and revolvers if lucky, all the light artillerymen had to fight back with were very curved, brass-hilted sabres. The sabres, due to the great curve, were unpopular and if sabres were carried at all they tended to be cavalry sabres.

As befits such soldiers, light artillerymen wore a unique dress uniform. Trousers and fatigue uniforms, as well as officers' uniforms, were the same as the infantry, but for dress they wore a tall, wool-covered leather shako, bound on top and bottom with shiny leather, with a leather visor. A red worsted cord hung from side to side with a tassel at each end. A brass crossed-cannon badge, with the regimental number below the X-shape of the crossed guns and battery letter above was worn under a brass eagle plate. Above the eagle was a large plume of red horsehair. From the left top button, where the cord ended in a tassel, a long red worsted cord hung down, coming down the back and under the arm and being buttoned to the third button from the top of the man's

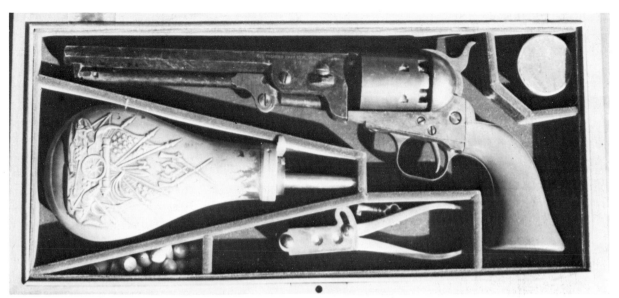

Colt Navy 0·36-calibre revolver in case, with powder flask, bullet mould, caps and bullets. (Author's collection)

jacket. From that hung two large worsted inter-woven circular tassels.

The jacket they wore was defined in regulations as '. . . of dark blue cloth, with one row of twelve small buttons on the breast placed at equal distances; stand-up collar to rise no higher than to permit the chin to turn freely over it, to hook in front at the bottom, and to slope the same as the coat-collar; on the collar, on each side, two blind button-holes of lace, three-eighths of an inch wide, one small button on the button-hole, lower button-hole extending back four inches, upper button-hole three and a half inches; top button and front ends of collar bound with lace three-eighths of an inch wide, and a strip of the same extending down the front and around the whole lower edge of the jacket; the back seam laced with the same, and on the cuff a point of the same shape as that on the coat, but formed of the lace; jacket to extend to the waist, and to be lined with white flannel; two small buttons at the under seam of the cuff, as on the coat cuff; one hook and eye at the bottom of the collar. . . .' Lace was red, as were N.C.O.s' chevrons, trouser stripes and officers' shoulder-straps. As with all other coats, brass shoulder-scales were to be worn on the jackets. Dress hats were rarely worn, but the jackets were popular and worn in the field throughout the war.

Officers of heavy and light artillery, as indeed all officers, had the same basic uniform as infantry officers. According to 1861 regulations, however, 'A round jacket . . . of dark blue cloth, trimmed with scarlet, with the Russian shoulder-knot, the prescribed insignia of rank to be worked in silver in the centre of the knot, may be worn on undress duty by officers of Light Artillery'. These jackets, without the Russian shoulder-knots but with standard straps, were widely worn by all mounted officers, and some dismounted ones as well. They were highly popular with officers of the last combat branch, the cavalry.

The Cavalry

Although some 272 cavalry regiments were raised throughout the war by the Union Army, it took longer to develop the city-dwellers of the North into good, serving field cavalrymen than into troops for any other branch. At the war's beginning there were five U.S. regular cavalry regiments, the 1st and 2nd Dragoons, the Mounted Rifles and the 1st and 2nd Cavalry, each regiment of five squadrons of two troops each. Early in 1861 the 3rd Cavalry was authorized and another squadron was added to each regiment. A bit later the designations were changed, making them all cavalry regiments numbered from one to six.

Each troop was to be made up of 100 men, with

A 20-lb rifled Parrot gun

a captain, a first lieutenant, a second lieutenant and a supernumerary lieutenant, known as the 'third' lieutenant. In 1863 the cavalry was re-organized, putting from 82 to 100 men in each troop and eliminating supernumerary officers. The squadron was eliminated and men were formed into battalions of four troops each.

A regiment included a colonel, a lieutenant-colonel, three majors, an adjutant, a quarter-master, a commissary, and a regimental surgeon and his assistant. There was also a sergeant-major, a quartermaster-sergeant, a commissary sergeant, a saddler sergeant, a chief farrier (blacksmith) and two hospital stewards. Each troop, besides its officers, had a first sergeant, a quartermaster-sergeant, five sergeants, eight corporals, two teamsters, two farriers, one saddler, a waggoner and two musicians.

It was one thing to take volunteers and organize them into cavalry regiments like the regulars – it was quite another to make them good cavalrymen. A captain of the 10th New York Cavalry wrote about his troop mounting their horses for a long march after six weeks of service: 'Many of the men had extra blankets, nice large quilts presented by some fond mother or maiden aunt (dear souls), sabers and belts, together with the straps that pass over the shoulders, carbines and slings, pockets full of cartridges, nose bags and extra little bags for carrying oats, haversacks, canteens, and spurs . . . curry-combs, brushes, ponchos, button tents, overcoats, frying-pans, cups, coffee-pots, etc. . . . but my company had hardly time to get into proper shape when "the general" was sounded, "boots and saddles" blown.

'Such a rattling, jingling, jerking, scrabbling, cursing, I never heard before. Green horses – some of them had never been ridden – turned round and round, backed against each other, jumped up or stood like trained circus-horses. Some of the boys had a pile in front of their saddles, and one in the rear, so high and heavy it took two men to saddle one horse and two men to help the fellow into his place. . . . Some of the boys had never ridden anything since they galloped on a hobby horse, and they clasped their legs close together, thus unconsciously sticking their spurs into their horses' sides. . . . Blankets slipped from under saddles and hung from one corner; saddles slipped back until they were on the rumps of horses; others turned and were on the underside of the animals; horses running and kicking; tin pans, mess-kettles . . . flying through the air.'

Soon the novice cavalrymen learned that Uncle Sam had given them quite enough to carry and little from home would be needed.

The cavalryman's burden began with his uniform, starting with a felt hat like that worn by the infantry, only with a pair of crossed sabres instead of the *Jäger* horn and a yellow hat cord and tassels. His dress jacket was the same as the light artilleryman's, only with yellow lace instead of red. Indeed, all coloured markings, such as officers' shoulder-straps, N.C.O.s' chevrons and trouser stripes, were yellow in the cavalry.

Trousers were sky-blue with a heavy insert sewn into the seat and inside legs, so that riding would not wear them out as quickly as regular trousers. Mounted light artillerymen had the same reinforced trousers. Shoes were issue for all other ranks, but both mounted artillerymen and cavalrymen tried to get boots where possible.

The cavalryman was the most completely armed of all Union soldiers. He was issued an 'Army' revolver which was worn in a black holster, butt towards the front, on the right side of his waist-belt. A small leather cap-box was next to that and often he wore a small pouch for pistol

1 Sergeant, 7th New York State Militia, 1861
2 Private, 6th U.S. Infantry Regiment, 1861
3 Corporal, 1st Rhode Island Regiment, 1861

MICHAEL YOUENS

A

1 Private, 39th New York Regiment, 1861
2 Corporal, 3rd U.S. Artillery, 1861
3 Private, 3rd New Jersey Cavalry, 1862

B

1 Lieutenant, 5th New York Regiment, 1862
2 Sergeant, 1st U.S. Cavalry, 1862
3 Sergeant, 14th Brooklyn Regiment, 1862

MICHAEL YOUENS

C

1 Private, 95th Pennsylvania Regiment, 1862
2 Captain, 2nd U.S. Artillery, 1862
3 Private, 1st U.S. Sharpshooters, 1862

D

1 Musician, 1st Maine Heavy Artillery, 1862
2 Lieutenant-Colonel, 9th New York Cavalry, 1862
3 Sergeant-Major, 42nd Pennsylvania Regiment, 1863

E

1 Private, 69th New York Regiment, 1862
2 Brigadier-General, 1863
3 Private, Ambulance Corps, detached from
the 41st New York Regiment, 1863

F

MICHAEL YOUENS

1 Chaplain, 14th Connecticut Regiment, 1863
2 First Sergeant, 4th U.S. Coloured Troops, 1864
3 Major-General, field dress, 1864

G

1 Private, 140th New York Regiment, 1865
2 Musician, 9th Regiment Veteran Reserve Corps, 1865
3 Private, 114th Pennsylvania Regiment, 1865

H

MICHAEL YOUENS

Artillery fuses, in different coloured wrappings according to times. (Author's collection)

ammunition behind it. From his left side hung his slightly curved, brass-hilted sabre in an iron scabbard. A wide black shoulder-belt, with a brass buckle at the rear, ended on the left side in a hook which was fastened to a carbine.

Carbines were usually breechloading, with a 0·52-calibre bore. They were rifled and fired Minié balls, although their range was shorter than full muskets. Later in the war the single-shot Sharps, Smith and Burnside carbines, to name three of the more popular models, were replaced where possible with the seven-shot Spencer.

Originally Union cavalry acted mostly as a screen for infantry, fighting dismounted with their carbines. Both the fact that they were yet untrained for traditional cavalry service and the fact that they were usually assigned in small units to infantry units created this role. As the war went on, however, Union cavalry gained both training and respect from the other branches and, more importantly, from the enemy. In October 1864 Confederate General Jubal Early wrote: '. . . the fact is the enemy's cavalry is so much superior to ours, both in numbers and equipments, and the country is so favorable to the operations of cavalry, that it is impossible for ours to compete with his. Lomax's cavalry is armed entirely with rifles and has no sabers, and the consequence is they cannot fight on horseback, and in this open country they

cannot successfully fight on foot against large bodies of cavalry.'

Another Confederate officer, a member of the Army of Northern Virginia's cavalry, said: 'During the last two years no branch of the Army of the Potomac contributed so much to the overthrow of Lee's army as the cavalry, both that which operated in the Valley of Virginia and that which remained at Petersburg.'

The Technical Corps

A corps which actually contributed as much as the cavalry, but received nothing like its praise, was the engineers. In 1861 there was both a Corps of Engineers and a Corps of Topographical Engineers, which were merged in 1863 to form an overall Corps of Engineers. The Topographical Engineer Corps was involved in drawing and producing the maps used by the army.

The entire Corps of Engineers had been reorganized on 3 August 1861 to consist of a colonel, two lieutenant-colonels, four majors, twelve captains, fifteen first lieutenants, fifteen second lieutenants, forty sergeants, forty corporals, eight musicians, 256 artificers and 256 privates – making forty-nine officers and 600 other ranks. The Topographical Engineers had only forty-two officers. By the war's end the regular army's Corps of Engineers consisted of 105 officers and 752 other ranks.

Besides the regulars there were two volunteer engineer regiments, the 15th and 50th New York Engineer Regiments, in the Army of the Potomac. Most engineering work was done by them, the regulars or infantrymen assigned temporary duty as engineers. Each infantry regiment had men assigned to this duty permanently, called pioneers, who were marked by a cloth badge of crossed hatchets in sky-blue worn on each sleeve.

Engineers wore the same basic infantry uniform, with yellow for the corps' colour. On their black dress hats they wore a brass castle, with a sally-port in front and turrets at each end – still the badge of the U.S. Corps of Engineers today. In the

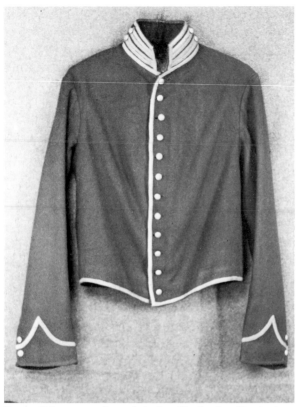

Front of the mounted man's jacket. (Author's collection)

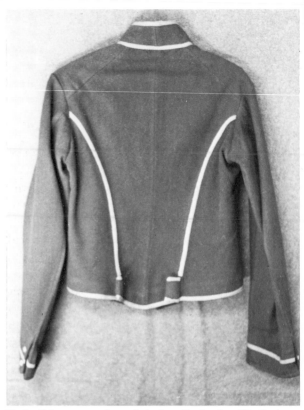

Back of the mounted man's jacket. (Author's collection)

field, judging from photos of engineers in the Army of the Potomac, they wore the plain fatigue uniform. However, according to regulations, they were allowed a white cotton '. . . garment to cover the whole of the body below the waist, the breast, the shoulders, and the arms; sleeves loose, to allow a free play of the arms, with narrow wristband buttoning with one button; overalls to fasten at the neck behind with two buttons, and at the waist behind with buckle and tongue'.

While the Topographical Engineers were eliminated, in August 1864 a new corps, the Signal Corps, was authorized. Commanded by Major A. J. Meyer, the originator of the army's signal system, the corps had some 300 officers and 2,500 other ranks in it. Signals were passed on mainly by flags, torches, rockets, flares and telegraph – the latter being the most important system. Despite its importance in signalling, however, in the Union Army the telegraph was operated by the United States Military Telegraph Corps, part of the Quartermaster's Department. Men who worked the telegraphs were civilian employees, not soldiers, although the job was

dangerous enough. In fact, one out of every twelve operators was wounded, captured, killed or died in prison.

Another civilian-run operation was the Balloon Corps, an informal organization headed by a famous civilian balloonist, Thaddeus Lowe. It served, in order, under the Corps of Topographical Engineers, the Quartermaster's Department, the Corps of Engineers, and, finally, the Signal Corps. The Signal Corps had neither men nor money to maintain the balloons and, after Chancellorsville the Balloon Corps was unfortunately disbanded.

Balloonists sometimes wore the brass letters 'B.C.' (Balloon Corps) or 'A.D.' (Aeronautic Department) on their hats, but these were non-regulation and discarded after they took some ribbing from the other soldiers about them. Signal Corps men were detached from line units and wore their old uniforms. During the war, however, the Signal Corps adopted a badge with two crossed signal flags – basically the same badge worn by the corps today.

The Medical Service

The corps that members of all the other corps probably had the strongest emotions about – for or against – was the Medical Department. At the war's start there were 115 men in it, of whom twenty-seven resigned to join the Confederate Army. Throughout the war the regular Medical Department remained small.

Each regiment brought with it a surgeon and assistant surgeon, who were part of that regiment and rarely detached for hospital service. Some of these men were good doctors, others best described as 'quacks'. Later the Medical Department cracked down on unqualified surgeons and this problem was largely eliminated.

More medical assistance was needed and on 3 May 1861 a surgeon was added to each brigade. These men were staff-surgeons, with the rank of major, and considered equals to the regular Medical Department's surgeons, when acting as medical directors of armies, corps or departments or in charge of hospitals. As well as the staff-surgeons, there was a group called acting assistant surgeons, who were actually civilian doctors hired by contract to work in specific hospitals.

Surgeons wore the same uniform as their equal officer rank in the other branches. Their shoulder-straps were green, as was their sash. Because of this difference, surgeons seemed to keep their sashes throughout the war even when most officers abandoned theirs. An infantry regimental commander in the wilds of South Carolina in March 1863 recalled being '. . . joined on the way by our . . . surgeon . . . his green sash looking quite in harmony with the early spring verdure of those lovely woods'.

As the wounded grew in number, hospitals grew to serve them. Congress on 3 August 1861 'added to the medical staff of the army a corps of medical cadets, whose duty it shall be to act as dressers in the general hospitals and as ambulance attendants in the field, under the direction and control of the medical officers alone. They shall have the same rank and pay as military cadets at West Point.'

Medical cadets also wore officers' uniforms. Their shoulder-straps were 'a strip of gold lace three inches long, half an inch wide, placed in the middle of a strap of green cloth three and three-quarter inches long by one and one-quarter inches wide'. They wore green sashes and forage-caps.

Other ranks who served in hospitals were hospital stewards. In rank they were placed somewhere between a sergeant-major and a first sergeant, and wore the frock-coat with crimson trim on collar and cuffs. Their trousers had a crimson strip $1\frac{1}{2}$ inches wide on each leg. Their black dress hats had buff and green mixed cords and tassels, with a brass wreath in front, with the letters 'U.S.' in Roman type made of white metal in the middle of the wreath. Like all non-commissioned officers, they were to wear a 'red worsted sash, with worsted bullion fringe ends; to go twice around the waist, and to tie behind the left hip, pendant part not to extend more than eighteen inches below the tie'.

In the field, however, the principal badge of the hospital steward was his '. . . half chevron of the following description, – viz.: of emerald green cloth, one and three-fourths inches wide, running obliquely downward from the outer to the inner seam of the sleeve, and at an angle of about thirty degrees with a horizontal parallel to, and one-eighth of an inch distant from, both the upper and lower edge, an embroidery of yellow silk one-eighth of an inch wide, and in the centre a "caduceus" two inches long, embroidered also with yellow silk, the head toward the outer seam of the sleeve'.

Before, however, the wounded soldier could get into the helpful hands of the surgeon, medical cadet and hospital steward, he had to be removed from the battlefield. Originally the regimental musicians or whoever else happened by were to remove the wounded and put them on any available ambulance heading towards the rear. Such a plan was faulty, at least, and when Dr Jonathan Letterman was named Medical Director of the Army of the Potomac he set up a new system in orders dated 2 August 1862.

He set up a field-hospital system, based on the

Typical cavalry guidon. (Smithsonian Institution)

division level, with a surgeon in charge, with an assistant surgeon acting as executive officer and another assistant surgeon as recorder. Three surgeons were the operating staff, aided by three assistant surgeons. This pooled supplies at that level and put the best available men in their proper jobs. (This basic structure served the U.S. Army until after the Second World War.)

Then he set up an Ambulance Corps of permanently detached men, trained in their duties. Each division ambulance train was commanded by a first lieutenant, with a second lieutenant for his assistant. The train's other ranks consisted of a sergeant for each regiment, three privates – a driver and two stretcher-bearers – for each ambulance and a private for every wagon. The train itself would be made up of from one to three ambulances for each regiment, squadron or battery, with a medicine wagon for each brigade and a couple of supply wagons. The surgeon-in-chief of the division commanded both the hospital and ambulance train.

At times three or more division hospitals would be consolidated and commanded by a corps medical director, aided by the medical inspector, quartermaster, commissary and chief ambulance officer. In combat temporary depots were set up as near as possible to the line of battle where the wounded would be taken first. As soon as their wounds had been superficially treated, they were sent on to the division or corps hospital. These would also be established close to the front lines, usually just out of enemy artillery range.

To prevent men from line units accompanying wounded men back just to escape enemy fire, ambulance-train men were given distinctive badges. On 2 August 1862 it was ordered: 'The uniform for this corps is: For privates, a green band 2 inches broad around the cap, a green half chevron 2 inches broad on each arm above the elbow, and to be armed with revolvers; non-commissioned officers to wear the same band around the cap as a private, chevrons 2 inches broad and green, with point toward the shoulder, on each arm above the elbow.' On 24 August 1863 these orders were revised. 'This corps will be designated: For sergeants, by a green band $1\frac{1}{4}$ inches broad around the cap, the chevrons of the same material, with the point toward the shoulder, on each arm above the elbow. For privates, a band the same as for sergeants around the cap, and a half chevron of the same material on each arm above the elbow.'

The Army of the James, which joined the Army of the Potomac at Cold Harbor, Petersburg and the final campaigns, had slightly different markings for its ambulance corps: 'The uniform or distinctive badge of this corps shall be, for private and non-commissioned officers, a broad red band around the cap with a knot upon the right side, and a red band, one inch wide, above the elbow of each arm.'

To guide the ambulance men and wounded to help, the hospitals were marked with special flags. On 4 January 1864 they were ordered to have flags of yellow with a large green 'H' in the centre. All ambulances were to have flags of '. . . yellow bunting fourteen by twenty-eight inches, with a border, one inch . . . of green'. Ambulance flags were also stuck into the ground along the way to field hospitals to mark the paths.

Corps Insignia

As the army grew larger – 2,763,670 men served throughout the war in the Union armed forces – still more badges had to be devised to tell one organization from another. In March 1862 the

Carbine cartridge-box; pouch in front is for patches and tools. (Author's collection)

Army of the Potomac was divided into corps, and Major-General Philip Kearny ordered officers of his 1st Division, III Corps, to wear a patch of scarlet cloth on their hats. Kearny was a favourite of his men, and the other ranks, too, adopted this as a badge of honour, which set them apart from the rest of the army. The cloth is said to have been cut from overcoat linings.

Kearny was later killed in battle, and on 4 September 1862 the division's new commander ordered: 'As a token of respect for his memory, all the officers of this division will wear crêpe on the left arm for thirty days, and the colors and drums of regiments and batteries will be placed in mourning for sixty days. To still further show our regard, and to distinguish his officers as he wished, each officer will continue to wear on his cap a piece of scarlet cloth, or have the top or crown-piece of the cap made of scarlet cloth.'

Kearny probably picked red because on 24 March 1862 each division was ordered to have a flag, red for each 1st Division, blue for each 2nd Division and red and blue for each 3rd Division – all flags being 6 feet by 5 feet.

At any rate, the idea of special badges was a good one. On 21 March 1863 Major-General Joseph Hooker, commanding the Army of the Potomac, issued the following circular:

'For the purpose of ready recognition of corps and divisions of the army, and to prevent injustice by reports of straggling and misconduct through mistake as to their organizations, the chief quartermaster will furnish without delay the following badges, to be worn by the officers and enlisted men of all the regiments of the various corps mentioned. They will be securely fastened upon the center of the cap. The inspecting officers will at all inspections see that these badges are worn as designated.

'First Corps – a sphere: red for First Division; white for Second; blue for Third.

'Second Corps – a trefoil: red for First Division; white for Second; blue for Third.

'Third Corps – a lozenge: red for First Division; white for Second; blue for Third.

'Fifth Corps – a Maltese cross: red for First Division; white for Second; blue for Third.

'Sixth Corps – a cross: red for First Division; white for Second; blue for Third. (Light Division, green.)

'Eleventh Corps – a crescent; red for First Division; white for Second; blue for Third.

'Twelfth Corps – a star: red for First Division; white for Second; blue for Third.'

Hooker felt the system was important and on 12 May 1863 he ordered that the '. . . badges worn by the troops when lost or torn off must be immediately replaced', and that 'Provost-marshals will arrest as stragglers all other troops found without badges, and return them to their commands under guard'.

Actually badges were highly popular and not always just worn on hats. Fancy metal ones, painted the correct colours and even silver for 2nd Divisions, were bought and worn on the left breast. Corps badges were also worn on dress hats and even forage-caps on the left sides. III Corps artillery used a badge of a large diamond, broken into four smaller diamonds. These were coloured red, white and blue, with two of the small diamonds being the correct colour for the wearer's division. They, too, were usually worn on the cap's left side and not the top.

On 24 March 1864 the old I Corps, worn by battles, was merged into the equally worn V Corps, and the V Corps badge was supposed to be worn by all men in the new V Corps. Many of the former corps, wishing to retain the traditions of their old badge, wore a badge made up of a I Corps circle round a V Corps Maltese cross.

Cavalry usually fought dismounted, one man for every four horses left in the rear

Other corps took up the practice of corps badges: IV Corps, which had been created on 3 March 1862 and stood down on 1 August 1863, never had a badge, but IX Corps had quite an elaborate one. On 10 April 1864 the corps was ordered to wear a badge made up of 'a shield with the figure nine in the center crossed with a foul anchor and cannon, to be worn on the top of the cap or front of the hat'. The corps commander and his staff had badges of 'red, white, and blue, with gilt anchor, cannon and green number'. The corps had four divisions and the badges were to be, in order, red, white, blue and green.

Such a badge was rather ornate – Tiffany's in New York City made the original badges in gold bullion – and a bit hard for the other ranks to obtain. Therefore on 23 December 1864 orders read: 'All officers and enlisted men in this command will be required to wear the Corps Badge upon the cap or hat. For the Divisions, the badges will be plain, made of cloth in the shape of a shield – red for the first, white for the second, and blue for the third. For the Artillery Brigade, the shield will be red, and will be worn under the regulation cross cannon.' Officers' badges had garlands of thirteen stars and oak leaves added to the top and bottom borders of the shield respectively at that time.

Corps badges were popular and have been found on the sides of canteens and musket butts – anywhere, in fact, that soldiers could put them.

A corps which had no special badge was the Veteran Reserve Corps. This was organized on 28 April 1863 as the Invalid Corps and placed under command of the Provost-Marshal-General. Originally it was to have had three battalions, of which '. . . recruits of the 1st Battalion should be capable of using a musket: those of the 2nd Battalion are to have the use of one of the upper extremities; those of the 3rd Battalion are to have the use of at least one of their lower extremities'. Since there were not enough recruits for the 3rd

Battalion, no companies were organized for that battalion. While originally only disabled men were to be recruited, eventually men whose enlistments had expired and who were willing to continue serving, but not in front-line situations, were accepted for the corps.

Accordingly on 18 March 1864 the Invalid Corps' title was changed to that of the Veteran Reserve Corps.

The first uniform, ordered on 15 May 1863, included a 'Jacket: of sky-blue kersey, with dark-blue trimmings, cut like the jacket of U.S. cavalry, to come well down on the loins and abdomen'. On 29 May 1863 officers were to have a uniform consisting of a sky-blue frock-coat with dark blue velvet collar and cuffs, dark blue velvet shoulder-straps and sky-blue trousers with a double half-inch-wide stripe of dark blue down each leg. The sky-blue uniforms were unpopular and eventually officers were allowed to wear the same uniform as the rest of the army.

The use of men who previously would have been discharged was a symbol of how the U.S. Army had succeeded in converting itself from a small, highly professional group of Indian fighters to a huge force, made up of civilian volunteers and conscripts, able to take on and beat possibly the toughest opponent Americans have ever had to fight – other Americans.

MAJOR ACTIONS OF
THE ARMY OF THE POTOMAC

1861
Ball's Bluff, Va., 21 October: 15th, 20th Mass.; 40th N.Y.; 71st Pa.; Battery 'B', R.I. Arty.

1862
Big Bethal, Va., 4 April: III Corps
Siege of Yorktown, Va., 5 April–3 May: II, III, IV Corps
Seven Pines and Fair Oaks, Va., 31 May–1 June: II, III, IV Corps
Seven Days' Retreat, 26 June–1 July: I, II, III, IV, V, VI Corps; Cavalry Corps; Corps of Engineers
Second Bull Run, 30 August: Hooker's and Kearny's Div., III Corps; V Corps; Reynolds's Div., I Corps; IX Corps; also I, III Corps, Army of Virginia

Top, tintype of a mounted man in its case (Author's collection). Above, period tintype cases of gutta-percha with patriotic motifs (Author's collection)

Antietam, Md., 17 September: I, II, V, VI, IX, XII Corps; Couch's Div., IV Corps; Pleasonton's Cavalry Div.
Fredericksburg, Va., 13 December: I, II, III, V, VI, IX Corps

1863
Chancellorsville, Va., 1–4 May: I, II, III, V, VI, XI, XII Corps
Beverly Ford and Brandy Station, Va., 9 June: 2nd, 3rd, 7th Wisc.; 2nd, 33rd Mass.; 6th Maine;

86th, 104th N.Y.; 1st, 2nd, 5th, 6th U.S. Cav.; 2nd, 6th, 8th, 9th, 10th N.Y. Cav.; 1st Md. Cav.; 8th Ill. Cav.; 3rd Ind. Cav.; 1st N.J. Cav.; 1st, 6th, 17th Pa. Cav.; 1st Maine Cav.; 3rd W. Va. Cav.

Gettysburg, Pa., 1–3 July: I, II, III, V, VI, XI, XII Corps; Cavalry Corps

Culpepper, Va., 13 September: 1st, 2nd, 3rd Div., Cavalry Corps

Bristoe Station, Va., 14 October: II Corps; part of V Corps; 2nd Cav. Div.

Mine Run, Va., 26–28 November: I, II, III, V, VI Corps; 1st, 2nd Cav. Divs.

1864

Wilderness, Va., 5–7 May: III, V, VI, IX Corps; Cavalry Corps

Spottsylvania Court House, Va., 8–18 May: II, V, VI, IX Corps; Cavalry Corps

Yellow Tavern, Va., 11 May: 1st, 3rd Divs., Cavalry Corps

Siege of Petersburg, Va., 15 June on: II, V, VI, IX Corps; also X, XVIII Corps, Army of the James

1865

Hatcher's Run, Va., 5–7 February: III, V Corps; 1st Div., VI Corps; 2nd Cavalry Div.

Five Forks, Va., 1 April: V Corps; 1st, 2nd, 3rd Cavalry Divs.; Cavalry Div., Army of the James

Fall of Petersburg, Va., 2 April: II, VI, XI Corps; XXIV Corps, Army of the James

Sailor's Creek, Va., 6 April: II, VI Corps; Cavalry Corps

Appomattox Court House, Va., 8–9 April: Cavalry Corps; XXIV Corps and 1 div. XXV Corps, Army of the James

Surrender of the Army of Northern Virginia, 9 April: Army of the Potomac

ORGANIZATION OF THE ARMY OF THE POTOMAC AS OF APRIL 1862

HQ: 2 coys., 4th U.S. Cav.; 1 coy., Oneida Cav. (N.Y.); 1 coy., Sturgis Rifles (Ill.).

Provost Guard: 2nd U.S. Cav., 8th and 17th U.S. Inf.

Cavalry Reserve: 1st Brigade: 5th and 6th U.S., 6th Pa. 2nd Brigade: 1st U.S., 8th Pa., Barker's Squadron of Ill. Cav.

Artillery Reserve: Batteries 'K', 'G', 'E', 1st U.S.; Batteries 'A', 'M', 'E', 2nd U.S.: Robertson's Battery, 2nd U.S.; Batteries 'L', 'M', 'C', 'G', 'F', 'K', 3rd U.S.; Batteries 'G', 'K', 4th U.S.; Batteries 'A', 'I', 'K', 5th U.S.; Batteries 'A', 'B', 'C', 'D', N.Y. Arty. Bn. Artillery troops with siege-train: 1st Conn. Heavy Arty.

Engineers: Companies 'A', 'B', 'C', U.S. Engineers; 15th N.Y. Engineers; 50th N.Y. Engineers.

I CORPS

Cavalry: 1st, 2nd, 4th N.Y.; 1st Pa.

Unattached: 2nd Regt. U.S. Sharpshooters.

1st Division. 1st Brigade: 1st, 2nd, 3rd, 4th N.J. 2nd Brigade: 16th N.Y., 27th N.Y., 5th Me., 96th Pa. 3rd Brigade: 18th N.Y., 31st N.Y., 32nd N.Y., 95th Pa. Artillery: Battery 'D', 2nd U.S.; Battery 'A', Mass. Arty.; Battery 'A', N.J. Arty.; Battery 'F', 1st N.Y.

2nd Division. 1st Brigade: 1st, 2nd, 5th, 8th Pa. Reserve Regts. 2nd Brigade: 3rd, 4th, 7th, 11th Pa. Reserve Regts., 1st Pa. Reserve Rifles. 3rd Brigade: 6th, 9th, 10th, 12th Pa. Reserve Regts. Artillery: Battery 'C', 5th U.S., Batteries 'B', 'C', 1st Pa.

3rd Division. 1st Brigade: 2nd, 6th, 7th Wisc., 19th Ind. 2nd Brigade: 20th N.Y.S.M.; 21st, 23rd, 25th N.Y. 3rd Brigade: 14th N.Y.S.M.; 22nd, 24th, 30th N.Y. Artillery: Battery 'B', 4th U.S.; Battery 'D', 1st R.I.; Battery 'A', N.H. Arty., Durrell's Pa. Battery.

II CORPS

Cavalry: 8th Ill.; 1 Squadron, 6th N.Y.

1st Division. 1st Brigade: 5th N.H., 81st Pa., 61st N.Y., 64th N.Y. 2nd (Irish) Brigade: 63rd N.Y., 69th N.Y., 88th N.Y. 3rd Brigade: 52nd N.Y., 57th N.Y., 66th N.Y., 53rd Pa. Artillery: Batteries 'A', 'C', 4th U.S.; Batteries 'B', 'G', 1st N.Y.; Battery 'A', 2nd N.Y.

2nd Division. 1st Brigade: 2nd N.Y.S.M., 15th Mass., 34th N.Y., 1st Minn. 2nd Brigade: 69th, 71st, 72nd, 106th Pa. 3rd Brigade: 19th Mass., 7th Mich., 42nd N.Y., 20th Mass. Artillery: Battery 'I', 1st U.S.; Batteries 'A', 'B', 'G', 1st R.I.

III CORPS

Cavalry: 3rd Pa.

Men in typical fatigue dress, the lead one wearing a greatcoat, queue up for supper in a winter encampment

1st Division. 1st Brigade: 2nd Me., 18th Mass., 22nd Mass., 13th N.Y., 25th N.Y., 1st U.S. Sharpshooters. 2nd Brigade: 14th N.Y., 4th Mich., 9th Mass., 62nd Pa. 3rd Brigade: 17th N.Y., 83rd Pa., 44th N.Y., Stockton's Mich. Vols., 12th N.Y. Artillery: Battery 'K', 5th U.S.; Battery 'C', R.I. Arty.; Batteries 'C', 'E', Mass. Arty.

2nd Division. 1st Brigade: 1st, 2nd, 3rd, 4th, 5th Excelsior (N.Y.). 2nd Brigade: 1st Mass., 11th Mass., 26th Pa., 2nd N.H. 3rd Brigade: 5th, 6th, 7th, 8th N.J. Artillery: Battery 'H', 1st U.S.; 4th N.Y. Battery; 6th N.Y. Battery; Battery 'D', 1st N.Y.

3rd Division. 1st Brigade: 57th Pa., 63rd Pa., 105th Pa., 87th N.Y. 2nd Brigade: 38th N.Y., 40th N.Y., 3rd Me., 4th Me., 3rd Brigade: 2nd, 3rd, 5th Mich., 37th N.Y. Artillery: Battery 'G', 2nd U.S.; Battery 'B', N.J. Arty.; Battery 'E', R.I. Arty.

IV CORPS

1st Division. 1st Brigade: 67th N.Y. (1st U.S. Light Inf.), 65th N.Y. (1st U.S. Chasseurs), 23rd Pa., 31st Pa., 61st Pa. 2nd Brigade: 98th Pa., 102nd Pa., 93rd Pa., 62nd N.Y., 55th N.Y. 3rd Brigade: 2nd R.I., 7th Mass., 36th N.Y. Artillery: Batteries 'C', 'D', 'E', 'F', 1st Pa.

2nd Division. 1st Brigade: 5th Wisc., 49th Pa., 43rd N.Y., 6th Me. 2nd Brigade: 2nd, 3rd, 4th, 5th, 6th Vt. 3rd Brigade: 33rd N.Y., 77th N.Y., 49th N.Y., 7th Me. Artillery: Battery 'F', 5th U.S.; 3rd N.Y. Battery; Battery 'E', 1st N.Y., 1st N.Y. Battery.

3rd Division. 1st Brigade: 85th Pa., 101st Pa., 103rd Pa., 96th N.Y. 2nd Brigade: 85th N.Y., 98th N.Y., 92nd N.Y., 81st N.Y., 93rd N.Y. 3rd Brigade: 104th Pa., 52nd Pa., 56th N.Y., 100th N.Y., 11th Me. Artillery: 7th N.Y. Battery; 8th N.Y. Battery; Batteries 'A', 'H', 1st N.Y. Arty.

V CORPS

Cavalry: 1st Me., 1st Vt., 5th N.Y., 8th N.Y., 1st Mich., 1st R.I., Keye's Bn. of Pa. Cav., 18 coys. of Md. Cav., 1 squadron of Va. Cav.

Unattached infantry: 28th Pa., 4th Potomac Home Guards.

1st Division. 1st Brigade: 12th Mass., 2nd Mass.,

16th Ind., 1st Potomac Home Guard, 1 coy. of Zouaves d'Afrique (Pa. Vols.). 2nd Brigade: 9th N.Y.S.M., 29th Pa., 27th Ind., 3rd Wisc. 3rd Brigade: 28th N.Y., 5th Conn., 46th Pa., 1st Md., 12th Ind., 13th Mass. Artillery: Battery 'F', 4th U.S.; Hampton's and Thompson's Md. Batteries; Battery 'F', Pa. Arty.; Battery 'M', 1st N.Y.; Knapp's Pa. Battery; McMahon's N.Y. Battery.
2nd Division. 1st Brigade: 14th Ind., 4th Ohio, 8th Ohio, 7th Va., 67th Ohio, 84th Pa. 2nd Brigade: 5th Ohio, 62nd Ohio, 66th Ohio, 13th Ind., 39th Ill. 3rd Brigade: 7th Ohio, 29th Ohio, 1st Va., 11th Pa., Andrew Sharpshooters. Artillery: Battery 'E', 4th U.S.; Batteries 'A', 'B', 1st Va.; Batteries 'A', 'L', 1st Ohio.

ORGANIZATION OF
THE ARMY OF THE POTOMAC
AS OF APRIL 1865

HQ: Troops 'B', 'F', 'K', 5th U.S. Cav.
HQ Guard: 4th U.S. Cav.
Provost Guard: 1st Ind. Cav.; Coys. 'C', 'D', 1st Mass. Cav.; 3rd Pa. Cav., 1st Bn., 11th U.S. Inf.; 2nd Bn., 14th U.S. Inf.
Artillery Reserve: 2nd Me.; 3rd Me.; 4th Me.; 6th Me.; 5th Mass.; 9th Mass.; 14th Mass.; 3rd N.J.; Battery 'C', 1st N.Y.; Battery 'E', 1st N.Y.; Battery 'G', 1st N.Y.; Battery 'L', 1st N.Y.; 12th N.Y.; Battery 'H', 1st Ohio; Battery 'B', 1st Pa.; Battery 'F', 1st Pa.; Battery 'E', 1st R.I.; 3rd Vt.; Batteries 'C', 'I', 5th U.S.
Engineers: Battalion of U.S. Engineers; 15th N.Y. Engineers; 50th N.Y. Engineers.

II CORPS

1st Division. 1st Brigade: 26th Mich., 5th N.H. Bn., 2nd N.Y. Heavy Arty., 61st N.Y., 81st Pa., 140th Pa. 2nd (Irish) Brigade: 28th Mass., 63rd N.Y., 69th N.Y., 88th N.Y., 4th N.Y. Heavy Arty. 3rd Brigade: 7th N.Y., 39th N.Y., 52nd N.Y., 111th N.Y., 125th N.Y., 126th N.Y. Bn. 4th Brigade: 64th N.Y. Bn., 66th N.Y., 53rd Pa., 116th Pa., 145th Pa., 148th Pa., 183rd Pa.
2nd Division. 1st Brigade: 19th Me., 19th Mass., 20th Mass., 7th Mich., 2 coys. of 1st Minn., 59th N.Y., 152nd N.Y., 184th Pa., 36th Wisc. 2nd Brigade: 8th N.Y. Heavy Arty., 155th N.Y., 164th N.Y., 170th N.Y., 182nd N.Y. 3rd Brigade: 14th Conn., 1st Del., 12th N.J., 10th N.Y. Bn., 108th N.Y., 4th Ohio, 69th Pa., 106th Pa., 7th W. Va.
Unattached: 2nd Coy., Minn. Sharpshooters.
3rd Division. 1st Brigade: 20th Ind., 1st Maine Heavy Arty., 40th N.Y., 73rd N.Y., 86th N.Y., 124th N.Y., 99th Pa., 110th Pa. 2nd Brigade: 17th Me., 1st Mass., 5th Mich., 93rd N.Y., 57th Pa., 105th Pa., 141st Pa. 3rd Brigade: 11th Mass., 7th N.J., 8th N.J., 11th N.J., 120th N.Y.
Artillery Brigade: 10th Mass.; Battery 'M', 1st N.H.; 2nd N.J.; Battery 'C', 4th N.Y. Heavy Arty.; Battery 'L', 4th N.Y. Heavy Arty.; Battery 'B', 1st R.I.; Battery 'K', 4th U.S.

V CORPS

Escort: Coy. 'C', 4th Pa. Cav.
Provost Guard: 104th N.Y.
1st Division. 1st Brigade: 185th N.Y., 198th Pa. 2nd Brigade: 187th N.Y., 188th N.Y. 3rd Brigade: 1st Me. Sharpshooters, 20th Me., 32nd Mass., 1st Mich., 16th Mich., 83rd Pa., 91st Pa., 118th Pa., 155th Pa.
2nd Division. 1st Brigade: 5th N.Y. (Veteran), 15th N.Y. Heavy Arty., 140th N.Y., 146th N.Y. 2nd Brigade: 1st Md., 4th Md., 7th Md., 8th Md. 3rd Brigade: 3rd Del., 4th Del., 8th Del., 157th Pa., 190th and 191st Pa. (as one unit), 210th Pa.
3rd Division. 1st Brigade: 91st N.Y., 6th Wisc., 7th Wisc. 2nd Brigade: 16th Me., 39th Mass., 97th N.Y., 11th Pa., 107th Pa. 3rd Brigade: 94th N.Y., 95th N.Y., 147th N.Y., 56th and 88th Pa. (as one unit), 121st Pa., 142nd Pa.
Unattached: 1st Bn., N.Y. Sharpshooters.
Artillery Brigade: Battery 'B', 1st N.Y.; Battery 'D', 1st N.Y.; Battery 'H', 1st N.Y.; Battery 'M', 15th N.Y. Heavy Arty.; Battery 'B', 4th U.S.; Batteries 'D', 'G', 5th U.S.

VI CORPS

Escort: Coy. 'E', 21st Pa. Cav.
1st Division. 1st Brigade: 1st and 4th N.Y. (as one battalion); 2nd N.J., 3rd N.J., 10th N.J., 15th N.J., 40th N.J. 2nd Brigade: 2nd Conn. Heavy Arty., 65th N.Y., 121st N.Y., 95th Pa. 3rd Brigade: 37th Mass., 49th Pa., 82nd Pa., 119th Pa., 2nd R.I., 5th Wisc.
2nd Division. 1st Brigade: 62nd N.Y., 93rd Pa., 98th Pa., 102nd Pa., 139th Pa. 2nd Brigade: 2nd Vt., 3rd and 4th Vt. (as one unit), 5th Vt., 6th Vt.,

Guards of the 107th U.S. Coloured Troops in front of the guardhouse at Fort Corcoran. (Black Spear Historical Productions)

1st Vt. Heavy Arty. 3rd Brigade: 1st Me., 43rd N.Y., 49th N.Y., 77th N.Y., 122nd N.Y., 61st Pa. *3rd Division.* 1st Brigade: 14th N.J., 106th N.Y., 151st N.Y., 87th Pa., 10th Vt. 2nd Brigade: 6th Md., 9th N.Y. Heavy Arty., 110th Ohio, 122nd Ohio, 126th Ohio, 67th Pa., 138th Pa. *Artillery Brigade:* 1st N.J.; 1st N.Y.; 3rd N.Y.; Battery 'L', 9th N.Y. Heavy Arty.; Battery 'G', 1st R.I.; Battery 'H', 1st R.I.; Battery 'E', 5th U.S.; Battery 'D', 1st Vt. Heavy Arty.

IX CORPS
Provost Guard: 79th N.Y.
1st Division. 1st Brigade: 8th Mich., 27th Mich., 51st Pa., 37th Wisc., 38th Wisc. 2nd Brigade: 1st Mich. Sharpshooters, 2nd Mich., 20th Mich., 46th N.Y., 60th Ohio, 50th Pa. 3rd Brigade: 3rd Md., 29th Mass., 57th Mass., 59th Mass., 18th N.H., 14th N.Y. Heavy Arty., 100th Pa.
Acting engineers: 17th Mich.
2nd Division. 1st Brigade: 35th Mass., 36th Mass., 58th Mass., 39th N.J., 51st N.Y., 45th Pa., 48th Pa., 7th R.I. 2nd Brigade: 31st Me., 2nd Md.,

56th Mass., 6th N.H., 9th N.H., 11th N.H., 179th N.Y., 186th N.Y., 17th Vt.
3rd Division. 1st Brigade: 200th Pa., 208th Pa., 209th Pa. 2nd Brigade: 205th Pa., 207th Pa., 211th Pa.
Artillery Brigade: 7th Me.; 11th Mass.; 19th N.Y.; 27th N.Y.; 34th N.Y.; Battery 'D', Pa. Arty.
Cavalry: 2nd Pa.

INDEPENDENT BRIGADE: 1st Mass. Cav., 61st Mass. Inf., 80th N.Y. Inf. (20th N.Y.S.M.), 68th Pa. Inf., 114th Pa. Inf.

SELECT BIBLIOGRAPHY

Billings, John D., *Hardtack & Coffee*, Boston, 1888
Lord, Francis, *They Fought for the Union*, Harrisburg, 1961
Official, *U.S. Army Regulations*, Philadelphia, 1861
Wiley, Bell I., *The Life of Billy Yank*, Indianapolis, Indiana, 1951
Wiley, Bell I., and Milhollen, Hirst D., *They Who Fought Here*, New York, 1959

A detail of men of the 107th U.S. Coloured Troops. Note the shoulder-scales and white gloves. The men carry Model 1864 Springfields. (Black Spear Historical Productions)

The Plates

A1 Sergeant, 7th New York State Militia, 1861
The 7th New York was one of the most famous of the state militia regiments and one of the first to volunteer to go to Washington in 1861. It was almost more social in purpose than military, as were many pre-war militia regiments, and hundreds of men left its ranks to become officers in other volunteer regiments. Its gray uniform was typical of 1861 Union regiments.

A2 Private, 6th U.S. Infantry Regiment, 1861
The small regular army was the backbone of the huge volunteer army which was needed to crush the rebellion. The men, many of them long-service veterans, wore the regulation uniform and were proud of it and themselves.

A3 Corporal, 1st Rhode Island Regiment, 1861
Colonel, later Major-General, Ambrose Burnside formed the 1st Rhode Island and designed its uniform. The regiment wore blue pull-over smocks and undressed black felt hats. Their blankets were red wool, with a slit in the centre, designed to be worn like ponchos. Two companies were armed with carbines which Colonel Burnside designed himself.

B1 Private, 39th New York Regiment, 1861
The green dress of the 39th New York (Garibaldi Guard) was taken from the crack Italian corps of riflemen and sharpshooters, the Bersaglieri. The regiment had three all-German companies, three all-Hungarian companies, and a company each of Swiss, Frenchmen and Italians. The regiment turned in a good record, although its first colonel was cashiered and ended his career in the New York State prison at Sing Sing.

B2 Corporal, 3rd U.S. Artillery, 1861
The light artillery uniform was probably the fanciest of all regular uniforms, but rarely worn by anyone but regulars and then not at all in the field. The shell jackets, however, were popular and, minus shoulder-scales, did see field use.

B3 Private, 3rd New Jersey Cavalry, 1862
The 3rd New Jersey also referred to themselves as the 1st U.S. Hussars. Their dress was the issue shell jacket, with more yellow braid and two more rows of buttons added. Their caps were issue forage-caps with the brim and strap removed and much braid added. The rest of the army laughingly called them 'the butterflies'.

C1 Lieutenant, 5th New York Regiment, 1862
Uniform for zouave officers was somewhat plainer than for the men. Often the *kepi*, with some red and gold additions, was the only indication that the officer was in a zouave regiment. In a few regiments officers wore baggy trousers and short jackets like the men.

C2 Sergeant, 1st U.S. Cavalry, 1862
The regulation cavalry uniform was like the light artillery one, except that the hard felt hat was worn instead of the shako. Until all mounted regiments had been organized as cavalry, cavalry wore yellow trim, while dragoons wore orange, and mounted rifles green.

C3 Sergeant, 14th Brooklyn Regiment, 1862
The 14th Brooklyn was a pre-war militia unit and given a much higher number in the regular New York line. The regiment clung to its old 14th Brooklyn name, however, throughout the war. For the same reasons of unit pride they also retained their red trousers although most pre-war units ended up in standard Union fatigue dress.

D1 Private, 95th Pennsylvania Regiment, 1862
The 95th Pennsylvania (Gosline's Zouaves) began the war in a modified zouave uniform, with their trousers being less baggy than true zouave ones. As the fancy uniforms were worn out they were replaced with the regular fatigue sack coat, forage-cap and sky-blue trousers.

with breech-loading Sharps rifles. Officers had a cap-badge with a wreath and the Old English letters 'U.S.S.S.'

E1 Musician, 1st Maine Heavy Artillery, 1862
All musicians wore extra lacing on the fronts of their frock-coats or shell jackets, depending on their branch, of the correct colour. They also carried a straight sword like the N.C.O. sword, but lacking the guards on either side. Musicians in the regular army were trained on Governor's Island, New York, and a veteran recalled '. . . that the pupils, who were urchins from 13 to 15 years old, picked up for the most part in the streets of the large cities in the east, learned their beats by the beat of a rattan, for their howls could easily be heard through a good part of the island'.

E2 Lieutenant-Colonel, 9th New York Cavalry, 1862
The field officer was marked by two rows of buttons on his frock-coat. In the field the sash was rarely worn, save by the officer of the day.

Captain in the regulation single-breasted coat. (Author's collection)

D2 Captain, 2nd U.S. Artillery, 1862
All company-grade officers wore the same uniform, regardless of branch of service. The artillery officer was identified by the red stripe on his trousers and the red background to his shoulder-straps. Artillery officers often preferred boots, as they rode, while infantry officers liked shoes, since they walked. The artillery officer's issue sabre was a sharply curved weapon like the other ranks' issue sabre, with engraving on the brass guard. It was unpopular with all ranks, however, and cavalry sabres or foreign sabres, mostly British, were preferred.

E3 Sergeant-Major, 42nd Pennsylvania Regiment, 1863
The 42nd, recruited in the north-western part of the state, was enlisted as a rifle regiment. At first they received 0·69-calibre smoothbore muskets, but these were quickly replaced by the breech-loading Sharps muskets. By 1864 these had been again replaced by the seven-shot, magazine-fed Spencer rifle, one of the best weapons in Union hands.

F1 Private, 69th New York Regiment, 1862
The 69th, also known as Meager's Zouaves, was one of many all-Irish regiments in the Union Army. Most of the men were also active in the Fenians, a group dedicated to overthrowing the British government in Ireland, and considered the war as training for that future war. Many participated in the Fenian invasion of Canada in 1866, wearing the uniforms of the Union Army. At least one major meeting of Fenian leaders, both Union and Confederate, was held on neutral ground between the armies during the war to plot the war against Great Britain.

D3 Private, 1st U.S. Sharpshooters, 1862
Two regiments of U.S. Sharpshooters, also called Berdan's Sharpshooters, were formed. They wore the standard frock-coat and trousers, but made of rifle green and not blue wool. Their buttons were black hard rubber instead of brass. Their knapsacks were of hairy hide and they were armed

The soldier, about to have a problem with some bees, wears his forage-cap in a typical manner and a blanket roll instead of a knapsack

F2 Brigadier-General, 1863

The general officer was marked by his buff silk sash. His collar and cuffs were made of black velvet, as were the insides of his shoulder-straps. His official sword was a narrow, straight-bladed weapon with an ornately cast brass hilt.

F3 Private, Ambulance Corps, detached from the 41st New York Regiment, 1863

Early in the war musicians were ordered to carry wounded men to aid, but it was seen that a formal and trained organization was needed for the Ambulance Corps. Men wore a band round their caps and a half chevron on their arms to indicate service with that corps. New York provided special shell jackets for their men, trimmed in the corp's colours, and with small

buttoned tabs on each side to hold the waist-belts up. Pennsylvania provided, apparently, special five-button fatigue blouses to its men, but the New York jacket was the most elaborate state-issue uniform in the army.

G1 Chaplain, 14th Connecticut Regiment, 1863

While regulations spelled out a specific chaplain's uniform, there were more variations in what chaplains wore than between anyone else in the whole army. Chaplains equipped themselves and were often considered 'excess baggage' in the regiment, so were rarely taken to task for wearing non-regulation uniform. Generally, however, they seem to have worn dark blue or black frock-coats, often with black instead of brass buttons; dark blue trousers; a dark blue *kepi*, often with a gold cross and wreath in front. Most supplied themselves with straight swords and black belts with buckles with a cross-and-wreath motif. During the war the first Jewish chaplains were admitted to the service.

G2 First Sergeant, 4th U.S. Coloured Troops, 1864
There was no special identification to the dress of U.S. black troops. They seem to have made more of an effort to be perfectly regulation than white troops, probably more as a matter of special pride in the uniform and cause.

G3 Major-General, field dress, 1864
In the field general officers used the same coats they wore for dress, but more informally. Soft felt hats were usually preferred by generals and many even neglected to wear swords. The vest was common to them all, but was worn by many soldiers down to the lowest cannoneer.

H1 Private, 140th New York Regiment, 1865
Because of unique abilities, often at drill or in the field, some regiments were awarded zouave status even though they were formed as ordinary infantrymen. Such was the case with the 140th New York, whose uniforms were imported from France especially for them. Often French uniforms had to be resewn because they were too small for average Americans.

H2 Musician, 9th Regiment Veteran Reserve Corps, 1865
Colonels were fairly free to make additions to their bands' uniforms as they wished. The 9th added dark blue braid and shoulder-tabs to their regulation sky-blue shell jackets. Their shakos are French infantry shakos, with a special Americanized brass badge in front.

H3 Private, 114th Pennsylvania Regiment, 1865
One of the new zouave regiments both to begin and end the war in zouave dress was the 114th Pennsylvania, Collis's Zouaves. The regiment served on the headquarters guard of the Army of the Potomac during the final campaigns, which may explain how their dress was so well protected. The regiment even had special brass cap-box plates issued them, as well as waist-belt and cartridge-box plates.